# Where Did Mommy Go?

*This book is dedicated to those who lost their battle to addiction:*
*Robert James Seely, Rande Carol Maynes, John David Seely, and Morgan Steven Seely.*

## Where Did Mommy Go?
### HELPING KIDS COPE WHEN A PARENT GOES INTO TREATMENT

**Copyright © 2020 by Kandace Marugg. All Rights Reserved.**

No part of this publication may be reproduced, stored in a retrieval system or transmitted, in any form or by any means—electronic, mechanical, photocopying, recording or otherwise—without prior written permission from the publisher, except for the inclusion of brief quotations in a review.

For information about this title or to order other books and/or electronic media, contact the publisher: Amaranth Press, LLC, 5123 W. 98th St. #1081, Minneapolis, MN 55437
website: amaranthpress.net, email address: contact@amaranthpress.net

AMARANTH PRESS

**ISBNs:**
978-0-9980317-6-7 (hardcover),
978-0-9980317-8-1 (softcover)
978-0-9980317-7-4 (eBook)

Publisher's Cataloging-in-Publication Data
Names: Marugg, Kandace, 1993- author.
Title: Where did mommy go? : helping kids cope when a parent goes into treatment / Kandace Marugg.
Description: Minneapolis : Amaranth Press, 2020. | Summary: Spooks the cat is worried because her mommy is going away for a while to a treatment center so she can get better. | Audience: Ages 3-5.
Identifiers: LCCN 2020946094 (print) | ISBN 978-0-9980317-6-7 (hardcover) | ISBN 978-0-9980317-8-1 (paperback) | ISBN 978-0-9980317-7-4 (ebook)
Subjects: LCSH: Picture books for children. | High interest-low vocabulary books. | CYAC: Cats--Fiction. | Family problems--Fiction. | Substance abuse--Fiction. | BISAC: JUVENILE FICTION / Social Themes / Drugs, Alcohol, Substance Abuse. | JUVENILE FICTION / Family / General. | JUVENILE FICTION / Readers / Beginner. | JUVENILE FICTION / Animals / Cats.
Classification: LCC PZ7.1.M37 Wh 2020 (print) | LCC PZ7.1.M37 (ebook) | DDC [E]--dc23.

Printed in the United States of America

Cover and Interior design: Kathryn Lloyd | Editing: Shannon Ruhl | Illustrations: I Kadek Yogi Pranata

First Edition

10 9 8 7 6 5 4 3 2 1

# Where Did Mommy Go?

## Helping Kids Cope When a Parent Goes Into Treatment

### by Kandace Marugg

This is Spooks the cat.

This is Spook's mommy and daddy, Stella and Tom.

Spooks and her mommy and daddy
would drink milk together.
She noticed Mommy would drink
a strange kind of milk.

Afterward, Mommy sometimes acted weird. She would talk funny and not be able to walk straight.

Then Mommy would get tired
and fall asleep before Spook's bedtime.

One evening when Daddy was saying goodnight to Spooks, he told her that Mommy would be going away for a while.
Spooks asked, "Why?"
Spook's daddy smiled. "Mommy is going to a special place to get better so she won't drink her strange milk anymore."

A few days later, Daddy took Mommy to the treatment center. Grandma came to stay with Spooks. Mommy said, "Don't worry Spooks. I will be home soon and you can come visit me. I love you."

Spooks spent a lot of time with Daddy while Mommy was away.

Spooks missed Mommy,
but she talked to her on the phone
every day.

Daddy took Spooks to visit Mommy at the treatment center where she was getting better. Spooks liked to see Mommy, even if it was just for a while.

Thirty days went by and Mommy was finally coming home. Spooks was excited! Spooks could tell that Mommy looked much better now that she didn't need her strange milk.

That evening, Mommy tucked Spooks
into bed and gave her a kiss
on the forehead.

Spooks went to sleep that night knowing that she, Daddy, and Mommy would be a stronger and happier family now.

The End

# My Personal Tips:

## How to Talk to Your Child About Your Visit to a Treatment Center

1. **Choose a good time to talk.** Sit close to eye level with your child. Choose a time and place with no distractions and when you don't feel rushed.

2. **Speak honestly** about what is going on. Let your child know that you are going away to get better, and that it is best for your health.

3. **Be respectful** of the child's boundaries and feelings. Speak in easy to understand and age-appropriate terms. Also, be respectful when speaking about the other parent involved. It's okay to be truthful with a child about an addicted parent's problem, just make sure to stay positive and avoid negative remarks.

4. **Explain how long** you (or the other parent) are going to be gone.

5. **Contact while you're away:** Make sure the child understands that they will talk with you on the phone and that they can come visit you at the treatment center.

6. **Get feedback.** Ask the child if they have any questions. Encourage them to talk about their feelings with you or another trusted adult. Provide resources.

7. **Feeling safe.** Make sure your child feels safe with the person who will be caring for them while you are in treatment.

8. **Plan fun activities** for them to do to help pass the time while you're gone.

9. **Speaking to a therapist:** Ask if they would like to talk with another grown-up.

10. **Addiction is a disease.** Make sure the child understands their parent is sick, not bad.

*Where Did Mommy Go?*

# Resources for Families:

## Hotlines:

1. Substance Abuse and Mental Health Service Administration (SAMHSA):
   1-800-662-HELP (4357)
   SAMHSA's National Helpline is a free, confidential, 24/7, 365-day-a-year treatment referral and information service (in English and Spanish) for individuals and families facing mental and/or substance use disorders.

2. National Youth Crisis Support:
   1-877-968-8491
   If a child is in crisis or is concerned about their safety.

3. National Association for Children of Alcoholics (NACoA):
   1-888-55-4COAS (1-888-554-2627)
   This national nonprofit organization works on behalf of children of alcoholics.

4. National Youth Crisis Hotline:
   1-800-448-4663
   Crisis help for youth and teens.

5. Recovery Centers of America:
   1-866-843-2642
   Alcohol and drug addiction treatment in your neighborhood.

# Resources

## Meetings:

1. Al-Anon® and Alateen® meetings:
   https://al-anon.org/al-anon-meetings/find-an-al-anon-meeting
   Al-Anon and Alateen are Twelve Step Programs to help those affected by someone else's drinking.

2. Alcoholics Anonymous® (AA):
   https://www.aa.org
   AA is a Twelve Step Program for alcoholics.

3. Narcotics Anonymous® (NA):
   https://www.na.org/meetingsearch
   NA is a Twelve Step Program support group for any kind of addiction.

4. Adult Children of Alcoholics® (ACoA):
   https://adultchildren.org/meeting-search
   Adult Children of Alcoholics (ACA)/Dysfunctional Families is a 12-Step, Twelve Tradition program of men and women who grew up in dysfunctional homes.

## Websites:

1. Substance Abuse and Mental Health Service Administration (SAMHSA)
   https://www.samhsa.gov/underage-drinking/parent-resources
   Resources for parents to help start—and keep up—the conversation about the dangers of drinking alcohol and using other drugs at a young age.

2. Sesame Street in Communities:
   https://sesamestreetincommunities.org/topics/parental-addiction
   Children's activities, printables, videos, tips, and more.

3. National Association for Children of Alcoholics (NACoA):
   https://nacoa.org/resources
   http://www.nacoa.net/kidspage.html
   For children and family members affected by addiction.

4. The Hazelden Betty Ford Children's Program:
   https://www.hazeldenbettyford.org/treatment/family-children/childrens-program/resources
   Helpful resources and activities for children affected by addiction.

5. Psychology Today:
   https://www.psychologytoday.com/us/therapists
   Find a therapist in your area.

6. Changing Minds NOW:
   https://changingmindsnow.org
   Information and resources for trauma in kids.

7. Child Mind Institute:
   https://childmind.org/our-impact/trauma-response/guides
   Free, multilingual downloads of Child Mind Institute resources to help communities in the wake of tragic events

# About the Author

Kandace Marugg is a licensed alcohol and drug counselor in Minnesota. As a child of alcoholic parents, along with her little brother, she lost her father to a drug overdose and was taken away from her mother, who was also an addict. She grew up with her grandparents, but later lost her mother to a heroin overdose. Kandace pledged to become an alcohol and drug counselor to help put families back together.

Kandace started her counseling journey in Washington State and worked at an intensive outpatient treatment facility for two and a half years. When her fiancé's job required them to move, they traveled to Minnesota and she began counseling men at inpatient facilities in Waverly and Elk River, but later found her counseling home at a residential facility for women in St. Paul.

The women she counseled were worried because their children were too young to understand what was going on and why their parent had gone into treatment. Then, driving home from work one day, a story idea came to her and Kandace was inspired to write this book. The main character is actually based on her real-life cat named Spooks.

Printed in the USA
CPSIA information can be obtained
at www.ICGtesting.com
LVHW071910031123
762894LV00020B/1006